Resilient
REAL ESTATE
WOMEN

8 Successful Real Estate Women
Share Their Current Best
Thinking And Key Strategies
For Inspired Leadership
And For Growing
A Profitable Real Estate Business

WM

Resilient Real Estate Women

First published in March 2021

WM Publishing

ISBN 978-1-912774-75-3 Pbk

ISBN 978-1-912774-74-6 eBk

Editors: Kim Hayden & Andrew Priestley

Cover art Angela Merzib brand strategist BeBoldBranding

The rights of Leigh Brown, Michelle Bailey, Sarah Johnston, Christina Swyers, Dr Lee Davenport, Kat Drerup, Mary-Anne Gillespie and Kim Hayden to be identified as contributing authors of this work have been asserted in accordance with Sections 77 and 78 of the Copyright Designs and Patents Act, 1988.

A CIP catalogue record for this book is available from the British Library.

All rights reserved. No part of this book may be reproduced in material (including photocopying or storing in any medium by electronic means and whether or not transiently or incidentally to some other use of this publication) without the written permission of the copyright holder except in accordance with the provisions of the Copyright, design and Patents Act 1988. Applications for the Copyright holders written permission to reproduce any part of this publication should be addressed to the publisher.

Disclaimer: *Resilient Real Estate Women* is intended for information and education purposes only. This book does not constitute specific legal, financial, health, clinical or commercial advice unique to your situation.

The views and opinions expressed in this book are those of the authors and do not reflect those of the Publisher and Resellers, who accept no responsibility for loss, damage or injury to persons or their belongings as a direct or indirect result of reading this book.

All people mentioned in case studies have been used with permission, and/or have had names, genders, industries and personal details altered to protect client confidentiality.

Contents

5 **Leigh Brown**
Foreword: A Career Unlike Any Other

11 **Kim Hayden**
Welcome to Resilient Real Estate Women

13 **Michelle Bailey**
Learning My Place

29 **Sarah Johnston**
Adventures In Teal Estate: Finding Balance And Flattening The Curve

39 **Christina Swyers**
A New Era Of The Female Realtor

53 **Dr Lee Davenport**
Resilient Real Estate Woman Know How To TAP Into (FREE) Their Value

67 **Mary-Anne Gillespie**
Mindset Matters

81 **Kat Drerup**
Unlock Your Best Life:
Turn A "No" Into A "Yes"
95 **Kim Hayden**
Roadmap To Success
105 **Invest In Yourself**
107 **About Real Resilient Tour**
109 **Would You Like To Contribute To Future Editions Of Resilient Women?**

Foreword: A Career Unlike Any Other

Leigh Brown

Resilient women in real estate – there's no other kind of woman in real estate that makes it more than five minutes in this business. What's fascinating to me is that these professionals, these entrepreneurs that you're going to hear from in this book, they didn't have to do real estate.

Now, there are many things in our lives that we have to do:

- We have to make sure that supper is on the table for our families.
- We have to get the bills paid.
- We have to take a shower in the morning.
- We have to work out.
- There are lots of have-to's in life.

But... we get to do real estate. When we get to do real estate, we get to be a part of somebody else's story.

These women get to have a CAREER, unlike any other career, that's part of somebody else's future – their financial future. They've supported themselves as independent women trying to make it in the world and not just trying but succeeding because we live in the greatest country on Earth, where we get to be entrepreneurs, and we get to do real estate.

What makes them resilient?

They understand this: they know that the job we perform in real estate is absolutely an honor.

People tell us things they wouldn't tell anybody else – because they know that we're going to give them our resilience. When that moment comes that we're going to help them find a way through any challenge or struggle, we're all in with them. That we can give them a little bit of energy to make it through because we know that real estate is the cornerstone of a great financial future for each of the people we serve, and it winds up serving us too.

Now, this doesn't mean that these resilient women who get to do real estate haven't had challenges and struggles. In fact, they'll tell you all of the times they failed. Because each of them knew that a failure was just a different stepping stone on the path, they go forward regardless and don't just lead the way for themselves, but they create opportunities for you who are reading this book. Those of you hope to learn ideas and get energy and come behind them to leave this path wider, brighter, and better than it was before any of us got here!

So thank you for picking up this book. Thank you for leaning into the stories of these women leaders. All I ask of you is that you take a nugget of wisdom from each of them and take it forward into the world so that somebody else can gain a little bit of energy from your resiliency.

Remember, none of us are in this alone.

We're only alone if we forget that there are others out there in the path with us.

About Leigh Brown

Leigh Brown, CEO, One Community Real Estate®, with over 20 years' experience in the real estate industry has successfully led her team to consistently be one of the top teams in North Carolina.

Leigh has served her profession as a volunteer on the local, state, and national levels since 2012. She was 2017 President of the Residential Real Estate Council, 2018 Chair of the REALTOR® Political Action Committee (RPAC) Trustees for Fundraising, 2019 RPAC Fundraising Liaison, and in 2020 Leigh joined the National Association of REALTORS® Executive Committee. She has served on the Advisory Board Member for the REALTORS® Relief Foundation since 2018 and will serve as the National Association of REALTORS® Vice President of Advocacy in 2021.

In addition Leigh serves her local community as a board member of Habitat for Humanity, Harrisburg's YMCA, and the NC Housing Finance Agency.

Leigh continues her mission to support and develop REALTORS® who are both leaders and advocates in their own communities while still striving to serve buyers and sellers as their REALTOR® advocate.

Contacts And Links

Website:
https://www.leighbrown.com

Facebook: leighbrownspeaker
https://www.facebook.com/LeighBrownSpeaker

Instagram: leighthomasbrown
https://www.instagram.com/leighthomasbrown

LinkedIn: leighthomasbrown
https://www.linkedin.com/in/leighthomasbrown

Twitter: leighbrown
https://twitter.com/LeighBrown

Youtube: leighbrownspeaker
https://www.youtube.com/leighbrownspeaker

Podcast: Crazy Sh*t In Real Estate
https://www.crazyshitinrealestate.com

https://podcasts.apple.com/us/podcast/crazy-sh-t-in-real-estate/id1153262163?mt=2

leigh@leighbrown.com

Welcome to Resilient Real Estate Women

Kim Hayden

Real estate is a demanding and rewarding business.

As a 21 year veteran and the mother of three children, I recognize the unique challenges that women in particular face in this industry. Challenges such as balancing the needs of our clients with the needs of our families, navigating ever changing societal expectations, and cultivating a leadership style amidst conflicting and often unfair, perceptions.

Did you know that while women in this industry make up 63% of all agents, they represent less than 30% of recognized leaders? This disparity is what inspired my quest to create a collaborative space focused on women in leadership.

One of my true joys in life is to explore and learn from the magic-makers of the world, and this book does just that. It brings together unique voices of women in real estate, each selected for their success and resilience.

They openly share their personal and professional stories, their key insights and their focused perspective aimed at inspiring and encouraging you on your own journey through real estate.

I know you will find these stories inspiring but you'll find them remarkably open and grounded.

This collection of wonderful stories covers a lot of ground and each author generously shares their current best thinking on growing and scaling a dynamic, profitable, high performing real estate business.

And truly succeeding at a deeply personal and fulfilling level.

I hope you get as much out of this book as I have in putting it together. Enjoy!

Resiliently Yours,

Kim Hayden

CEO/Founder Real Resilient Tour

Learning My Place

Michelle Bailey

Part of understanding someone's success is to understand their journey. We see ourselves in another person's journey or struggle, and we feel peace or acceptance in knowing that we are not the only ones. You might even say their story resonates with you.

My name is Michelle Bailey. I run a multi-million-dollar real estate business in Boise, Idaho. My business partner is Ben Kinney, one of the leading real estate business owners in the country. I coach agents and brokers all across the nation, and I volunteer in my local, state and national Realtor® associations.

In 2020, I served as president of the Boise Regional Realtors®- the largest Realtor® association in Idaho. I was inducted into the Realtor® Political Action Committee Hall of Fame for my level of investments in our industry.

Going forward, I will participate in the National Association of Realtors® Leadership Academy. I was one of 25 chosen for the program out of 200 applicants. Overall, 2020 has been a good year in spite of all the challenges of the global pandemic.

This success didn't happen overnight. I would even argue that it didn't happen fast enough. Just as when you give birth to a child, the days pass slowly, and then you look up and they are adults leading their own lives. That's how success generally happens-it's gradual, little by little, until all of a sudden, you're there!

I'll share some of my early story and what has led me to where I am today.

I was born 20 miles outside of San Francisco, California, in a town called Richmond. By the time I graduated high school, Richmond had a murder rate seven times higher than the national average. Although I don't know the exact demographics of the area when I lived there, I definitely felt like the minority. I was frequently teased, thrown against a wall, or picked on to incite a fight. This is when I first remember the feelings of "not being enough" and being labeled "white trash." I learned to hide my feelings, especially fear. I learned that words not only hurt me; I could use them to hurt back. It's also where I learned to lose myself in books. The public library was my haven. I could spend hours getting lost in any world I wanted.

I went to six different elementary schools, each time having to prove myself by being strong and hiding my fears.

To help my mom start a new life, my grandparents moved my mom, my sister, and me to Twin Falls, Idaho. That's where I spent my middle-school years.

I returned to California for high school. I thought I was going to live with my "rich" dad and enjoy a lavish lifestyle. For clarification, I never went without. I always had clothes, food and shelter. Unfortunately, life with my dad changed quickly. He divorced his second wife, his mom had a massive stroke and was left paralyzed until her death two years later, and he lost his business. The depression was too much to handle and he turned to drugs to help him cope. My sister and I would go days without seeing my father. However, we knew he was alive because of the dirty ice cream bowls left in the sink. I often felt I was living in two worlds. During the day, I lived like a typical teenager, involving myself in school and socializing with friends. At night, my life at home was quiet and depressing.

With the strong encouragement of a high school teacher, Leslie Davis, I attended Saint Mary's College of California in Moraga.

Once again, I was the "poor white girl" at a private, affluent college.

Due to this self-imposed mindset, I didn't take full advantage of the college scene. Instead, I found myself working two jobs and carrying a full load of classes. One of my jobs was working in the dispatch center of a police department. I worked the graveyard shift, going in at 9pm, and getting off at 7am, followed by a 45-minute drive, where I spent the rest of the morning in classes. I then drove home and slept until I had to get up and do it all over again. Once out of training, I found myself working up to 50 hours a week while still carrying a full load at college. I really liked the money! For the first time, it felt good to work hard and see the results.

But it came at a cost.

I no longer pushed to do what I originally wanted to go to school for (politics). I now attended school just to finish. My saving grace was my two roommates, Melissa and Andrea. We continued to live together through graduation, and they kept me connected to our friends at school. Looking back, I realize this job allowed me to play life safe. I didn't push to do anything outside of my new career. I didn't get out and meet new people, and I certainly didn't date as much as I could have.

After graduation, I decided to continue with my career in law enforcement. I worked for two more police departments and spent a few years with a company that sold public safety software. Regardless of where I worked, I always pushed to learn more and be the best I could be. During this time, I met my future ex-husband and father of my two sons. He was a police officer, and we actually worked together at the first and last department at which I was employed. It was at the last police department that I decided I didn't like where my life was headed. I was unhappy in my marriage and because of my work schedule, I couldn't be the mom I wanted to be. A year later, I decided to move back to Idaho and started a new life in Boise.

Getting into real estate was not my plan, but it's where I landed. Looking back, I don't know what I was thinking! Who moves to an area where they know almost no one and gets into sales with 100% commission as a single parent? I'm positive had I actually thought this through, I wouldn't be sitting where I am today. Thank goodness I didn't think about it! Back in those days, it was too overwhelming to think about long-term plans or how far I had to climb to get to the top of the mountain; I just focused on the next step in front of me.

I had success in the early days because I did what I had to do to survive. I didn't think about the obstacles. I focused on helping others and getting results.

My past life as a dispatcher set the groundwork for success in real estate. There are several skills I learned while dispatching that translated well to real estate.

- Dispatchers don't know all the answers but they know their resources and where to get the answers. Realtors are expected to know a lot about a lot of topics. They have to know where to refer their clients for answers to their questions.
- Dispatchers take complex situations and simplify them. Realtors break down the process of buying and selling into manageable steps and help their clients along the way.
- Dispatchers can read emotion and detect variations in someone's tone of voice. Realtors can read people and respond accordingly.

- Dispatchers don't respond from emotion; they respond with logic and they are the calm in the storm. Realtors handle all the urgent requests for information by clarifying questions allaying fears of first- time homebuyers and handling the stress of coordinating buying and selling at the same time.

- Dispatchers handle multiple priorities at once. Realtors juggle multiple buyers and sellers at the same time with contractual deadlines while finding new business and servicing current clients.

- Dispatchers ask questions until they get the answers they need. Realtors must dig deep to understand motivation in order to best serve their client and help keep them on the path.

Now back to the beginning of my real estate career.

It's 2006, and I'm a new real estate agent. I don't have a sphere, and I have no idea what to do. I joined a team that did Internet leads, just when Internet leads were becoming a thing. I didn't do a lot of research or evaluate who would give me the most for my money and I never asked about commission splits. Instead, I focused on business and how I was going to feed my family. I closed three deals my first five months in the business. My first deal was an Internet lead who told me he had an agent. After continuing to send him listings and following up, I found out his "agent" was someone in his office that wasn't answering his questions and wasn't showing him property. Follow up is key! Most agents only call once. Many will follow up two to three times. Most business happens between five to twelve follow-ups.

I was plugging along, doing what I could to get deals put together. I loved it, and I was seeing success!

In 2008 things changed.

The market slowed. There were more homes for sale than buyers and 60% of our sellers were in default. Of course, you know I'm referring to the Great Recession. I felt a little like a frog in boiling water. I didn't know I was in hot water until it was too late.

In 2009, I was helping many sellers with short sales on their own homes while helping them deal with the emotions of losing everything. Then it came time for me to do the same. I tried so hard to keep it together. I was working two other jobs in addition to selling real estate but it just wasn't enough.

In 2009, I had my broker short sell my personal residence; the only real home I had known since moving to Idaho. If there was ever a reason to stay in bed with the blankets pulled over my head, this was it! I was a failure. I couldn't support my children, the single most important job in my life and I failed. The self-talk at this time was powerful and defeating. I distinctly remember hiding in my bedroom closet of our new rental on Christmas Eve crying. I didn't want my children to see me at my lowest point.

Thankfully, that was my lowest point, and I was determined to not give up. I kept working, cleaned up my credit, put money in savings, and in three years

I was able to buy a home with an owner carry. During this time, I learned more about money and mindset. I taught Dave Ramsey's *Financial Peace* in hopes of helping others. I often met with sellers, and instead of listing their home, I helped them create a budget so they could afford to stay in their home. I began to realize the people I surrounded myself with mattered. I found myself discouraged and unmotivated when I spoke with other agents that talked about doom and gloom. Instead, I focused on solutions and helping people, and the business came.

In 2013, I made a decision to move to Keller Williams. Although I never asked about splits with my previous team, I couldn't imagine paying such a high cap (back then it was $21K). I had a mindset of scarcity. Now that I'd experienced failure and loss, I took longer to make decisions. I was so cautious that I overthought everything and added unnecessary stress to myself. I operated from fear! Operating from fear caused me to move at a snail's pace, and second- guess everything. I was a confident and successful Realtor®, but I actually felt like an imposter, about to be "discovered" at any moment.

Now here I am at Keller Williams as a solo agent, still the sole provider for my family and now understanding that everything starts and stops with me. Just as I had done in the beginning, I got into action. I started calling expired listings, past clients, buying my own Internet leads and working anything I could.

Soon I started building a team and making every mistake in the book!

In 2015, I hired an executive assistant, which would prove to be a game changer. I knew I had to hire Rebecca because I could tell she was going to push me. Not because that was her role, but because she scared me! She was emerging talent and I knew if I wanted to keep her I would need to show up differently. I would need to be the person I told her I was. I could no longer hide! Just to show you the caliber of person she was then and continues to be, her first day on the job was the day after my father passed away. Her first week on the job was without any direction from me. She created her own success!

I'm now business partners with Ben Kinney, one of the most successful real estate brands in the nation. Our team has increased 100% in revenue and continues to grow. I'm surrounded by leaders who scare me! They continue to push me, help me grow and challenge my thinking. I'm coaching others around the country and seeing their successes. My children are now grown and starting their own lives. And of course, I feel like mine is also just starting. It's a balance of hard work and enjoying the journey!

A few pieces of advice (in no order of importance):

- **Failure occurs when you stop trying.** Learn from your mistakes, get up, and try again.
- **Stop handling objections on the phone or via text.** Get in front of people! It's harder for people to say no when you are in front of them.
- **Be religious about your database!**

Put everyone you know in it and set them up on email campaigns. Find a way to keep in touch with them frequently. Add people to it every day.

- **Who you surround yourself with matters!** They are a direct reflection of how you see yourself. Do not underestimate the power of this. It's almost impossible to be a failure around successful people. You will either rise to the occasion or self-select to a new group.

- **Don't let ego get in your way!**

- **Do not compare yourself to others.** This isn't anything new and yet we still do this. Comparing yourself serves no one and will rob you of joy and celebrating your successes. Compare you to you!

- **Learn to say no.** Don't do things out of guilt or because you feel obligated. Remember when you say yes to something, you are absolutely saying no to something else.

- **Plan the night before.** My partner Ben created this success plan. The steps are listed below:

  - Visualize what you want to accomplish tomorrow.

  - See what your calendar has on it. Cancel what is not important.

  - Make a list of your priorities and put them in the right order. Start with the one thing you need to do to move your business forward, not a checklist of tasks for the day.

- Plan your rituals: water, meals, breaks, exercise, etc.
- Create a time block and set alarms for everything so you don't forget. Don't go longer than 90-120 minutes without a break.
- Sleep well knowing you have a plan.
- Wake up. Review the above and start the day in a powerful way.
- At the end of the day review what went well and what didn't. Make adjustments and start over the next day.

- **Don't be afraid to ask questions and dig deeper to understand your clients (or your agents).** You can better help them when you understand what they need. When they understand that you are there to help them, not just get a commission, they will open up more. Ask "What else?" or "What's important about that?" Be curious and genuine.

- **Make sure you have down time and thinking time in your schedule.** This includes vacations, weekends or evenings off. Make time for the important people in your life and be present with them. Don't over-schedule your day so you don't have time to think about your business. If you only work in your business, you will never discover what is needed to take your business to the next level.

- **Follow up, follow up, and follow up!** We often create stories around why someone isn't returning calls or emails. In reality, we all lead busy lives and often don't do something until we have to. Our clients are no different. If you have systems in place to keep yourself front of mind and then follow-up with consistent phone calls, you will get business.

- **Be honest with your word.** Not being honest doesn't serve anyone. Not telling your seller to clean their house doesn't help them sell. Not telling your buyer to get prequalified before looking at property only causes heartbreak and wastes time. Not being honest with an agent you're recruiting or coaching only leads to resentment and disappointment. It's hard having these conversations, but you are better off having had them.

Another important piece of the success equation is being coached by other successful people. These are my favorite podcasts:

- **Win-Make-Give with Ben Kinney**
  Winning in business and life; Leadership; Making the money we want to make and leaving a legacy.

- **The One Thing with Geoff Woods**
  All things about owning a business.

- **The Model Health Show with Shawn Stevenson**
  Health, exercise, mindset, etc. He's very well-rounded with his topics.

- **Entre Leadership (Dave Ramsey)**
  All things about owning a business.

- **Mark Groves Podcast**
  Mental health and relationships. I found him after a hard breakup and really enjoy his perspective and honesty.

- **Business Wars**
  How businesses came to be and how they have morphed through time to stay relevant
  or how they were replaced.

Over the years, I've found success in having routines and systems. John Maxwell says systems make the ordinary extraordinary.*

Find what works for you.

For example, I must work out consistently. I feel the stress and anxiety in my body when I don't. I love listening to podcasts and prefer them to books. I listen to them daily. I get at least seven hours of sleep a night, and I drink a gallon of water a day. It's important to have a plan, follow the plan, and make adjustments as needed. A plan takes us in a direction. Without direction we have no idea where we will land.

- *Maxwell, John. (Author, Speaker, Pastor). (2019, January 23)
  The Ordinary to Extraordinary Series (Audio Podcast)

About Michelle Bailey

In 2005, California native Michelle Bailey headed to Boise, Idaho, with her two young children. After having built a career in public safety, she realized that would not be her forever path. Characteristic of Michelle, she made an unconventional decision and dove headfirst into a real estate career.

She became a Realtor® in 2006 as a single mother, living in a new city, having zero sales history. She quickly made her mark, becoming a Broker in 2009, building a highly productive business, and garnering the attention of one of the country's top real estate business owners, Ben Kinney. This led to a 2016 partnership with Kinney and Bailey in Boise, which has grown into a multi-million dollar enterprise.

In 2019, she continued building her influence within the industry becoming a business coach with Forward Coaching. Michelle has coached both established real estate brokers as well as launching new Realtors® to hitting over $5M in sales production, within their first year.

Contacts And Links

Business website
https://michelle.bktboise.com

Facebook
https://www.facebook.com/michelle.vinesbailey

LinkedIn
https://www.linkedin.com/in/michellebaileyboise

Twitter @SellingIdaho

IG MichelleSellsIdaho

Adventures In Teal Estate: Finding Balance And Flattening The Curve

Sarah Johnston

It's been a little odd for me that 'flatten the curve' was the tagline of 2020. You wouldn't believe this, but it was actually my New Year resolution for the year! I mean, not in the 'worldwide pandemic' sense, because no one but Bill Gates could have predicted that. No, my resolution was to find the ultimate balance in real estate. You know, get off the roller coaster and flatten that curve! No more high highs or low lows. Nope, I was going to balance out the year no matter what the market did.

No more spending January and February doing yearly client home reviews, taking education class on top of on-line learning, and ordering all of my marketing for the year. Nope, because then March would then hit and you spend every waking hour trying to fill your schedule: taking calls, making appointments and running around town, only to realize that you might be carrying one too many listings. You slowly start to freak out in April when your inventory doesn't sell but then May hits. Oh May. Beautiful, beautiful May!

With the spring comes the flowers but more importantly, sales start to pick up!

So then on top of the calls, appointments and buying/listing errands; you now get to spend every meal eating alone in your coffee stained car while trying to sleep as little as possible, win or lose in multiple offers, and learn a new client management system (CRM), why do I always change my CRM in June?

Don't do that!

Those are the best six weeks of the year. Those weeks between mid-May and the end of June. I mean, I guess that really depends how you measure 'best'. Best for business but honestly, the worst for living. Cancel all of your plans and pray that your family needs for very little.

Want to go on a date? Don't bother.

Booked a trip? Cancel it!

Have a giant 50th birthday to plan? Ask your boyfriend to change his birth date, after all, we don't do those things until the summer!

Oh the summer. Sometimes they're fast, sometimes slow, but usually end up somewhere in the middle.

A trip can usually be planned here, but please, no longer than a week or two (I have heard of those going away for a month or more but I'm sure that's an urban myth passed down through the years). A slight uptick will occur after school starts again; I like to call it our 'second spring' (once again, prone to the dramatic), and then the slow wind down until winter. This is the time you replenish your marketing materials, change out your business cards, and get an 'after summer' professional photo taken while you still have a tan.

If you're REALLY lucky and have planned well, here is when you can spent a bit of time hauling three hundred dirty pumpkins around to your previous clients (please don't let them get too hot in the car, they WILL explode, or begin to decompose and smell oddly like dirty gym socks for the next two and a half months) and start preparing to write fifteen hundred Christmas cards (start those early, December 25th really sneaks up on you every year!).

Now, your market might be slightly different, but regardless of the economy, this has been the exact same cycle I have seen for the last 15 years.

IT'S EXHAUSTING!

Mind you, that's why we got into this business, isn't it? If we're exhausted then we must be successful! Don't the two go hand-in-hand? Pretty sure they do and I'm pretty sure that's what we've been telling ourselves for eternity. We just keep recreating that wheel!

So here's the thing, in 2020, I wasn't going to do this anymore! Not only was I not going to this, I had a plan to prove it!

You see, I take every course available. I'm an: Accredited Buyers Representative, a Certified Condominium Specialist, a Certified Negotiation Expert. Add a BSc. and a few others to this and I could put enough letters after my name to make an actual intellectual gag (and I would never do that because no one really cares that I can work with seniors or know how many gallons per minute is the prime water rate for a horse boarding facility).

I work on residential, commercial and rural properties, I've volunteered with my local board and spent 5 years climbing the ranks to Chair (ask me about governance in the not-for-profit real estate industry, I dare yah!). To top that all off, I've taken training!

All. The. Training.

From Tom Ferry to Richard Robbins, Larry Kendall (who I highly recommend), Brian Buffini (also great), and Grant Cardone. I also got into a habit of randomly signing up for free online courses, so I'm also an advertisers dream. Every real estate coach in the western hemisphere now has me on a drip email campaign.

So obviously, I had a plan! No more real estate roller coasters for me, nope, I was going to flatten that curve, have more time, and prove that there is a work life balance in real estate! *insert screaming and cheers here!!

Then 2020 showed up… and reminiscent of the housing collapse of 2008 - the joke was on me!

Don't worry, at first I was like everyone else. I went into a hardcore-melt-down-panic-mode. I came to terms that I wasn't going to sell another house again, and decided that 1,000 piece puzzles and showering every fourth day was my new life. But, somewhere during the second week of the first lockdown in March, I got bored.

That's when the training kicked in.

Instead of continuing to grow my paint-by-number collection, I went back to the basics! I went back to my daily schedule. I reached out to my clients and my network, asked how everyone was and provided things to do in lockdown. Have kids? Here's a coloring contest. Like to bake? Here's a sourdough recipe that I'm told won't fail (but I actually wouldn't know because I hate cooking). I continued marketing and continued working (although at this point, I also asked my Broker how long someone could possibly carry so many listings without any of them selling... still had to test my odds of complete failure).

You see, I wasn't prepared for the changes in 2008 but I sure learned from them. I mean, I was trained for the good years that preceded the collapse – who wasn't? It's easy to be outstanding when the market is hot. But it's not easy to be outstanding when the market is NOT.

2008 was a different time. The market collapsed, I actually did melt down (that was a fun five year journey of self-discovery and pain) and I vowed I would never go through that again. So while I wasn't prepared for the housing collapse of 2008, I've now realized that

I had prepared myself for market changes, economic collapses, and apparently, worldwide pandemics!

Yes, sure, you might be saying right now, "But Sarah, the market has been AMAZING where I am, this is nothing like 2008!"

And to you I say, perhaps! But what has this year prepared you for? Did you work the market, or did the market work you? How's your mental health? Are you feeling cool, calm, and collected or have you just now realized the amount of stress you've built up waiting for the other shoe to drop?

Let me guess, you stopped working in March, and then jumped immediately into to light speed through the summer. There may have been more clients, low inventory, multiple offers, and an exponential amount of running around. You were scrambling, and did everything you could to survive while worrying about the next day, the next deal, your family, your friends, getting sick, getting someone else sick, do you send the kids to school or not?

For a lot of agents around me, the market was either amazing or terrifying. We had either our best years ever or will carry lifelong scars. One thing was for sure though, there were no curves being flattened. Some people thrived and others barely survived (don't worry, both paths are normal right now!).

But here's where my path slightly altered… I actually met my 2020 goal. It surprised me too! I found balance and flattened that curve! I spent more time with my family, took more time off, sold more homes, worked harder in shorter periods of time, and for once I was able to not only plan a birthday party, but I even got to go to it! Oh yes, and my clients? I actually felt like I was finally on top of it all!

In a year that was as unpredictable as anything we have ever seen before, the lessons I learned in 2008 and onwards prepared me for something that was unheard of. In fact, I've noticed this with some of the top agents around me. When times change and balance seems unlikely, that's when your training kicks in! Survival mode as they call it, doesn't have to be merely about survival. It can be about so much more. Make your survival mode easy and it will also be automatic. When survival mode is automatic, you can create balance.

Sarah's Guide to Automatic Survival Mode

1. **Find a training program you like**: I prefer *Ninja Selling* by Larry Kendall, but that's because I like creativity and relationships. I'm not a fan of paying for online leads and want something with a bit of longevity. Whatever you do, please find a training program that gives you a schedule that you can stick to. You also have to like it. I have no idea why I've gone through full two week trainings for programs that are seriously not me. Don't do that! There is no need to get into the day to day minutia right now (you know, the business plans and marketing calendars – that's what the training program does!).

2. **Find a mentor or accountability partner(s):**
   While this person doesn't need to follow or teach in the same training program, make sure that their goals are aligned. There are a lot of different styles of agents, so please find one that feels right for you. If you like to learn lines and memorize scripts, great! If cold calling isn't your thing, then look elsewhere.
   There are a LOT of teachers out there! There are also a lot of agents that want to learn from each other.
   I had a *Ninja Selling* group that met every Monday for years. We learned so much from each other and although I've moved to another group now, it doesn't matter how successful you are - mentors and/or accountability partners are required for growth.

3. **Make learning a priority:** This is something that should never stop. One of the most amazing things to come out of 2020 are all of the free online tools and resources! They are everywhere.
   While I'm at it, learning includes reading, which should be done frequently. I'm a big fan of Audible so download a few new books a month. At the moment, my favorite (not so new) books are:
   Generating Business Referrals Without Asking by Stacey Brown Randall and *Outwitting the Devil, The Secret to Freedom and Success* by Napoleon Hill.

4. **Take care of your mental health:** Need a break? You best take it! Have you ever noticed how your communications take a nose dive when you need a break? I have a pretty easy litmus test for this. When my inside voice turns into my outside voice, I know I need a break (I actually just get far more

sarcastic than normal… it's a weird sarcasm meter.
If I hit 8, I need a break). These boundaries are the scariest ones though so here's what you say: 'I'm sorry, that weekend won't work for me. I take four days off in a row every month and that is my weekend.'
Everyone understands and then they think, 'Wow, you work really hard, and are worth waiting for!'
Mental health days, four day weekends, scheduled vacations, never, ever compromise on these!

I realize how simple and easy this sounds (and probably a little boring and phony), but trust me, it works! If you read something and it inspires you, that's great! But inspiration like motivation, both are fleeting. They'll last a few minutes, a few days, maybe a few weeks (highly unlikely), so instead of chasing motivation, learn a system and train! You don't need ALL THE THINGS! No one needs all the things. Find one thing. One idea. One mentor. Concentrate on one type of training or one coach! Find the idea that speaks to you or the coach that gets your language. Then? Follow it!

Don't let yourself get distracted with everything that's available. Make it easy or you'll never do it. I know we all feel as though we have to work long, hard hours and give up time with family and friends to feel successful, but that's an inherited lie that for whatever reason, we continue to perpetuate. They tell you that balance isn't possible in real estate. Well, they're wrong!

Put the time into training and balance will follow. Balance that will last you through any market condition!

About Sarah Johnston

Sarah Johnston is a 15 year veteran agent, Board President, Sarcastic Mentor, Swearer and Official Sharer of Ideas. From sharing her experiences and stories online to speaking in front of large crowds or meeting other REALTORS® for coffee, Sarah is trying to raise the bar of real estate. Her self-depreciating humour makes an easy entrance for anyone and has made her a fan favourite for nationwide podcasts and interviewers alike.

Of course, she has to have some downtime too and that is usually spent with her horse, dog, pretending to enjoy yoga or yelling at herself boyfriend on the golf course (she firmly believes that her bad shots are *his* fault).

Contact Sarah Johnston

@AdventuresInTealEstate

Instagram.com/adventuresintealestate

www.pinterest.ca/adventuresintealestate

ca.linkedin.com/in/sarah-johnston-1851ab72

sarahjohnston.ca

A New Era Of The Female Realtor

Christina Swyers

Who Am I?

Hi, I'm Christina Swyers, written in my most enthusiastic voice ever! I am a wife to my supportive husband and mother to three amazing sons. I live in the suburbs of St. Louis, MO. right in the heart of the Midwest.

I primarily help families buy and sell Real Estate, but I also love teaching them how to invest and build wealth through it. My goal is to help them along the process of the most expensive asset they will ever purchase, usually, and make sure they are educated and confident with me leading them to the finish line.

My clients work with me time and again because they know I value the relationship first. It's what has led me to become a successful trusted advisor and why I have been able to build a referral based social and digital media friendly business. I have created this business for myself around doing what I love, working with and serving others.

I have created a six figure a year business by utilizing unorthodox methods to what it is today.

In an age of Ring Doorbells and DO NOT CALL lists I have leveraged the power of social proof by showing up in my community and creating a brand around that.

Currently my accolades over a five- and half-year career include:

- Becoming the number one social media Realtor in St. Louis and number five in the state of Missouri.
- I have been featured in both Real Producers (rising star) and Top Agent (feature story) Magazines,
- I have sold over $23 million dollars of Real Estate locally,
- I am an ICON agent within my brokerage, EXP Realty, LLC. (less than two percent of Realtors currently are),
- I am a certified mentor of new agents, and
- I recently created a course to teach Realtors the art of branding and business building utilizing digital and social media.

When I am not selling houses or teaching agents, I love to give back through a local charity I am affiliated with called Connections to Success.

They help give socioeconomically challenged individuals hope through networking and mentorship to help them break their cycle of poverty.

Ever since I was a little girl, I can remember having this audaciousness about myself. Not necessarily reckless behavior, but definitely more like always wanting to see how far I could take something to get a response.

I have repeatedly made decisions out of listening to my intuition and that has served me very well.

I like making myself take risks and being a trailblazer. I think it stems as far back as I can remember at about two years old. It is wholeheartedly the result of being raised by parents who literally told me I was an amazing being who could do whatever I put my mind to. Even though they themselves did very few things outside of their comfort zones. My parents, who are still together 40 years later, raised me and my brothers in a typical middle-class family. I am the second oldest of five children and the only girl. I was rough and tough when I needed to be, a tomboy at times, but loved embracing being a girl and all things that came along with it including hair, makeup, girl scouts and my favorite passion-dancing. Throughout my youth I would spend hours upon hours at the dance studio. It instilled a confidence in me that has shaped the person I am and still carry with me today.

My Why

I should be a broke single mom on welfare. That was supposed to be my fate. Writing that now seems so surreal! If I am reminded of the pain that points towards lack in my life, I will run from that all day long.

I will do anything to stray. The current positivity in my life I have created wasn't always here. It has evolved to become part of who I am.

A choice if you will that stems from my personal experience of struggle and survival. The fear of not being able to provide for myself and my family is the absolute reason I work so hard. I never want to be reminded of where I was 23 ago.

I was a broke, single mom, on the verge of a breakdown and losing everything with no control over my life. I had my oldest son at the age of 20 and immediately remember having to grow up very fast.

I had to work a job I wasn't in love with while someone else was raising my child when I was away at work and I hated that.

Working for someone else, I had a boss telling me where to be, when I could take off work, or if I could go on vacation. IT SUCKED.

I craved more freedom. Looking back today I now know my motivation comes from wanting to be in more control of my day to day schedule.

I didn't need anyone else to motivate me. I was enough. My *why* has evolved from then to now though too.

I didn't realize how much I would love helping other Realtors with similar stories and struggles. I want to give all the mothers, especially single mothers, hope that you can have a thriving family and a bustling career. I know because I get to live this.

I want to motivate the person who might be where I was.

Part of my *why* now includes showing others what can be possible to overcome even if it's almost unseemingly impossible right now. This is the entire reason I share all my wins and losses and show up authentic, raw, and real.

Women don't need heroes; they need relatable role models. We all have gifts and talents.

Mine is to show the world that you need no one's permission to be whatever you want to be, to speak your truth and step into your purpose, but always remain loyal to your own personal vision of success.

The What

Learning to be a great Realtor hasn't always become easy for me, but it's because in the beginning I didn't really do my homework.

When I decided to get my Real Estate license, I had a kid in school and a baby on my hip. I was a stay at home mom who had left a seemingly successful corporate recruiting career. I truly learned a lot in my prior careers. Things that I still use on a daily basis.

How to read people, their body language, their tone, the psychology of building relationships to get someone to know, like, and eventually trust you.

Even before that I received an AAS in healthcare as a Radiology Technician. That career taught me empathy, compassion and kindness, but most of all it taught me humility. Throughout my twenties these career fields were preparing me for my life as a Realtor, I just didn't know it yet!

My first year in the Real Estate industry was still really tough. I almost got out of the business as fast as I got into it. I only sold three houses my entire first year. Ya I know.

What happened?

I was definitely motivated, but I didn't have direction or mentorship. I was also being taught in ways that were not a good fit for my personality. I didn't want to work phone duty, cold call, or door knock - I had done that for years in recruiting. Those ideals seemed outdated to me.

One thing that was fun for me was building relationships online with others. Social media became "my thing". There I could reach a massive and endless amount of people to build my brand. It just made sense.

I started posting my day to day experience so my sphere could see a day in the life of me! People loved that. I would consistently share my wins, you know, my just listed and just solds, but do it in a way that I could tell the story. I educated and asked questions to increase my engagement and my following as well.

I started showing up live and doing videos. I interviewed local businesses in my community and figured out a way to become a digital mayor in my town.

It worked. The leads started to come into my inbox and just haven't ever stopped. I became an authority in my market. I have had to pivot and change things up, but that is not just how the algorithm works, that's how life works.

If something is working keep doing it!

Along the way of my Real Estate career I have moved to a couple different companies. Recognizing a change is needed is really you listening to that inner voice.

I started at a big box franchise, switched to a boutique investment firm, and eventually landed at my current fit in a cloud-based brokerage. There isn't a one size fit's all approach, but I think listening to my intuition paired with having knowledge in a rapidly changing industry has helped me earn my success.

One thing that made me a bit rogue, but greatly helped my confidence was coming to EXP Realty. It has opened so many doors for me professionally that I didn't have prior and I have been mentored by so many amazing agents in our industry over the last three years. There is a right fit for everyone in this industry and this is mine.

Learning to ask for help by utilizing an assistant and/or a transaction coordinator and leveraging systems, like CRMs, have helped me grow and scale as a solo agent. The most important lesson I've learned in this business is that it takes time and patience to build this.

Wealth

Growing up in my family money was always tight. I watched my parents struggle. Even though our home held so much love, I remember this stress on my parents.

As I got older, I was never really taught how to save or spend right. I wasn't taught about how to use credit responsibly. I most certainly wasn't shown how to invest.

I was taught how to have a strong work ethic, how to always do the right thing, and how to show up no matter what. My parents worked very hard for everything we had, but we never got to experience things like regular family vacations.

Now, I obviously turned out OK, but I didn't realize how important those things would become to me once I had a family of my own.

I now make travel a very large part of mine and my family's lives. It's one of the ways I reward myself and spend quality time with my loved ones. That's a big part of what success looks like for me.

My message here is that it's OK for you to be content and happy with where you're at.

You don't have to find success and happiness in the same way that everyone else is creating it. It is completely okay to find that contentment when you have reached your personal level of success.

When I decided to get my Real Estate license this decision was based on a few things.

I wanted a career where I had more freedom in my day to day flexibility, I wanted to have no ceiling on my income, and I wanted to help others. That was my criteria and I made the decision to take massive action.

I know that wealth and success are not one and the same because wealth is measured in money and success is measured in subjective satisfaction, but to me the more wealth you are able to create and build, the more successes you are able to fulfill financially, personally, humanitarianly, etc.

I look at all the things I am able to do for and impact others when I am in abundance.

As I become more successful in my craft, I am able to give more of my time and add value to others to teach them to do the same. I am a big believer that when you give, the world has a funny way of exponentially giving back to you. That's not logic, just a bit of a faith driven message.

What's Your Worth?

We all have gifts and talents that stem from our deepest why's in life. Understanding what those are will help you become confident in showing others your value. There are many other things that I believe show my worth. I am proud to work for myself and run my business built my way.

It takes a whole lot of courage, perseverance, gumption, and grit. It takes an unwillingness to feel a bit crazy every day. It takes a belief in unrealistic things.

It takes a type of resolve that you didn't actually know lived inside of you until you need it. It takes more endurance than I can explain.

It is all so wildly worth it though.

Knowing all of this I know deep down you have to believe that you really are worth whatever you are asking for. You have to own it and communicate this effectively to others though.

As women, sometimes we make excuses as to why we can't or even worse we allow societal norms to make preconceived notions about what happens if we ask for our true worth. We have a tendency to put others before ourselves.

I have learned that strong women will find their backbone in this business or they will get eaten alive. The failure rate is so high in this profession because agents do not understand how to get others to see the value they bring.

Part of my success has been me being able to paint a picture for others through my words, my visions, my actions, my archetype, and my leadership.

Showing up isn't enough.

You must come across in your own authentic way just as you are. You must show others the way too. I live by the motto: *your network is your net worth* and truly believe you are who you surround yourself with. No one gets to the top alone. When you realize that this is a long game you are playing it will become easier to break down where you are and where you want to be.

Therefore, mapping out my goals has always helped me see my potential and my future in an underwhelming way. Personal development has helped give me the confidence at communicating my value to others.

I have poured years of time and thousands of dollars into self-development, coaching, books, courses, and retreats. I know that learning never stops, it just evolves with me. Asking for the sale and the rate you want is okay. Walking away from others who do not see your value is too. Hold steadfast in knowing that you are meant to serve others in a way that creates a sense of peace within you.

This is where your worth lies.

Wrap It Up!

There are lots of things I love to credit as being helpful to shape who I have become as a professional.

A few books that have really resonated with me and that I recommend are:

You are a Badass and *You are a Badass at Making Money*, both by Jen Sincero.

The 15 Invaluable Laws of Growth by John C. Maxwell, and *The Big Leap* by Gay Hendricks.

My favorite podcast is *Goal Digger* with Jenna Kutcher. Jenna is a female leader in branding, marketing, and social media.

One piece of advice I would give a brand-new Realtor would be to understand it takes a major level of patience and fortitude to build this business and it will not organically happen overnight.

Find a mentor, hire a coach, work smart, and show up every day.

Two quotes I live by are, *What we do in life echoes in eternity*, because I believe our imprint on this world never leaves, even after we are gone and *Nothing grows inside a comfort zone*, because success happens from failing forward.

About Christina Swyers

Christina Swyers is a top St. Louis, Missouri Realtor, social media influencer, and a digital mayor of her town. She has become a six-figure earner utilizing unorthodox career tactics to grow and scale her business and has taught many other professionals through her course content and direction. Working smart and having FUN are both mottos of hers! Christina was named the #1 Realtor on Social Media in St Louis in 2019 and the #5 Realtor on Social Media in Missouri in 2020. She has been featured in both Real Producers and Top Agent Magazines as their feature story.

Since 2015 she has belonged to both the National and St. Louis Associations of Realtors. She has served as a charity committee member at Connections to Success, currently holds her license with EXP Realty LLC, a cloud-based brokerage where she has become a certified mentor, ICON award agent, and is in the top 1% of EXP influencers. Christina is a wife to her husband Jeremy and mother to their three boys, Logan, Gage, and Benjamin.

Contacts And Links

www.Christinaswyers.com

Facebook @ Christina Swyers Living

Instagram @therealchristinaswyers

LinkedIn: Christina Swyers

Resilient Real Estate Woman Know How To TAP Into (FREE) Their Value

Dr. Lee Davenport

Uphill Battle To Real Estate My Way

Face-to-Face Impression: 'From your emails and your name, I thought you were a man! I probably wouldn't have worked with you if I had known otherwise.'

Truth: The US real estate industry is dominated by women so it does not take a man to succeed in real estate.

Face-to-Face Impression: 'All she is going to do is just open the door; we do everything else.'

Truth: As a real estate professional, I provide a wealth of value to the transaction beyond simply opening a door.

Face-to-Face Impression: 'You are too young to know what you are doing.'

Truth: I have a lifetime of experience as a proud second-generation real estate investor.

Face-to-Face Impression: 'She probably doesn't even have a college degree.'

Truth: I have a Bachelor's of Business Administration, a Juris Masters (Master's degree of legal studies that I had to use to write legal responses for company lawsuits), and a Doctorate of Business Administration as I have been a real estate investor, sales agent, managing broker and now educator/coach.

Sadly and shockingly, I have heard all of the above face-to-face comments (and worse) over the last 'twenty-ish' years in real estate, not from simply one or two uncouth maniacs that have no filters but from a majority of prospective real estate clients that I have personally met face-to-face.

In other words, I looked different than what they expected and they were not shy nor polite in telling me. Yet, many of them became clients and often long-term.

How is it possible that they were shocked when they met me in-person? Email and text messages can establish a faceless rapport, my dear Watson.

I have never hid how I look (like most real estate

professionals, my photo often precedes me). But, after corresponding with someone via email or text that had obviously not paid attention to my attached photo, they would take a liking to my straight-shooter style. I have been complimented often on the respectful yet firm tone my business emails conveyed, particularly prior to meeting in person for the first time.

Then there is the spelling of my first name, 'L-E-E' instead of what many deem the 'acceptable' spelling for a girl, 'L-E-I-G-H'.

I guess I am one of the few people that still remember the actresses 'Lee Meriwether' and 'Lee Remick'? (Perhaps I paid more attention to them because of their names, who knows?)

As a school girly girl, I despised having a name that mostly every new teacher mistook for a male, adding salt to my wound by over pronouncing 'Mr.' before reading my name or even doubling back to repeat 'Mr' twice. Whew, gender stereotypes were alive and well then!

And, since it was the 1980s, I was often taunted, 'Bruce Lee', which made me cringe to be called a man as a self-professed girly girl or 'Lee Jeans' after the fashion brand. Yet, as an adult, I reflect back and cherish being called a boss that made his own hodgepodge style (of marital arts) work like Bruce Lee and people speaking into existence my business brand.

Yes, I will take more of that positivity!

In truth, my parents lovingly named me 'Lee' in

honor of my precious grandfather, who was for most of his life an unsung Montford Point Marine of World War II (unsung until his corp received in 2012 the U.S. Congressional Gold Medal for serving in the military despite rampant discrimination and injustice just for being Black; he died from cancer in 2015 at the age of 89). Again, I did not then appreciate my first name's significance as a mildly teased 'tween. Now, however, it has been both a great honor to be the namesake of my favorite, 'Pop-Pop', and to eyewitness having a male-adjacent name open doors for me.

Even now as an educator, who has worked with firms and associations around the world, it never fails that some are in disbelief when they see me face-to-face. This is especially true if they had been copied on one of my strongly worded yet respectful emails.

But here is the thing. First impressions have never been able to define me (or defeat my drive) nor should they you. I am driven by my personal goals not others' personal opinions. Ultimately, achieving our goals (that should, in my opinion, reach each level of Maslow's hierarchy of needs) is my definition of wealth because quality of life (both money and contentment) cannot help but follow 'badassery'. I have been able to quantify my value (and help many sales agents do the same) in such a way that first impressions do not stick because they do not represent the truth, our truth.

As women in an industry that has a majority of women but is actually still skewed with male leadership, we have to be able to rise above stereotypes and misconceptions in order to quantify our value.

Men do it. For example, I have talked to men that have self-professed to struggling with imposter syndrome for a myriad of reasons. Yet, in the next breathe, they tell me how other men that have been in their position previously 'threw them a bone' by giving them different perspectives along with kind advice (a.k.a. informal mentorship) to help them build their sense of self-worth and self-confidence.

The result? These self-conscious men are able to take seats at negotiation tables without flinching and no one is none the wiser that they second-, third- or fourth-guessed themselves.

While often, we as women as a collective (particularly those of us that do not know the principle of quantifying our value that I share later in this chapter), are still notoriously known for not exuding confidence (a.k.a. standing our ground and demanding our value) when negotiating, particularly when the talks come to commission or salary.

But who can blame us if before we even open our mouths, we are being underestimated (and frankly verbally assaulted) like I have been with the first impressions I mentioned earlier?

No one.

The psychological tendencies of fight, flight, freeze or fawn (people-pleasing is a recognized defensive response too) kick in for most of us. But I propose we add a fifth response as resilient women and that is 'free'.

Instead of shrinking because of negativity, we can

expand and allow our value proposition to take up space and command our presence to be valued.

So let us 'free' our value together.

Rarely, does anyone gain true self-confidence (that is not obnoxious or arrogant) through osmosis. Typically, it takes mentorship that gives new information, which includes reading a book like this so kudos to you. I also recommend for this relationship-dominant industry the books *Emotional Agility* by Susan David, *The 10X Rule* by Grant Cardone, and *Profit with Your Personality* (my life's mantra) by yours truly (me) along with the podcasts *Small Things Often* from the Gottman Institute and *Unlocking Us* with Brené Brown'.

Law Of Goal Getters: T.a.p. Into (Free) Your Value

As a scientist at heart in a REALTOR's® body, I love to research, examine and discover why things work (or do not), especially for the agents that I coach. Furthermore, as a real estate coach and educator for over a decade, I have found one of the sure-fire ways for my sales agents to succeed in goal achievement is to be able to relentlessly not compromise on what they are worth.

Yes. I am referring to handling objections when it comes to your commission.

But no, I do not mean being a money bully or someone that gives off the slick, shyster, 'used car salesmen' vibes where you pull a fast one on a client, where she is left feeling like she just signed over her first-born.

I also do not mean we handle objections like the half comical, half reprehensible 1990s pharmaceutical drug commercials that tout all of the benefits with bells and whistles but in your best fast talking auctioneer imitation, you breeze past all concerning conditions.

There is a far more authentic and powerful strategy that works every time it is put into action fully. How do I know? I have had agents from places like Omaha to Singapore to the Caribbeans to San Francisco tell me how this principle works so well that not only do their prospects not question their commission but the prospects profess that the agent deserves more. MORE!

Specifically and notably, I even had a rookie Dallas agent share with me how her boyfriend wanted her to discount her commission for him. (Are you rolling your eyes too because he should know better?) I am sure many of you that have been in real estate sales for at least a couple of years can relate to family and friends (heck, even 'frenemies') wanting a steal and a deal when it comes to working with you. This newer Dallas agent used my principle below and her boyfriend wholeheartedly apologized. Then, to her surprise, he did a 180 degree turn and became her commission advocate with their other friends and family members who would become her clients.

Wow!

That needs to be recapped:

1. Agent used principle below to quantify her value,
2. Boyfriend paid full commission and
3. Boyfriend became her pro bono marketer without being asked.

Because of these consistent results, I dare call this principle a law.

I call this law, *T.A.P. into Your Value* because again we are quantifying why we belong in real estate spaces without for even a second diminishing our worth.

As a caveat, if you are new to real estate sales (what I consider two years or less), then you may need help doing the exercises and that is okay. Searching the internet, connecting with your broker or another local agent that has time to help is welcomed so that you can complete all of the columns. Just anticipate that as you come into your own stride in the real estate industry, you will want to update this assignment so that it accurately reflects how you serve clients in real estate.

The 'T' Stands For *Task*

We are in an industry that has thirty minute television shows sum up our work. 'Yay' for the exposure but 'boo' for the editing that cuts a process that may have taken weeks or months down to approximately 22 minutes. It is no wonder that those new to the the real estate sales process give us as sales professionals the side-eye when the first day they contact us they do not miraculously get the keys to their new dream home.

Real estate shows can definitely poison prospects minds but guess whose job it is to correct any misinformation? You got — it is ours. That is where the 'T' of *T.A.P. into Your Value* principle kicks in to play. For this item, please list every single task that you do for your clients. This is our opportunity to set the record straight on our terms. I would recommend creating separate lists based on buyers, sellers, landlords, and/or tenants.

This list is not for the faint at heart because the top producers I work with (those with an annual sales volume of $20 Million or more) typically have a list of 300 or more tasks they perform for clients.

That probably sounds overwhelming and it is supposed to be.

That is the power in this list because clients get to see that you actually do work overwhelmingly so, go figure. Newer agents, I want to challenge you to still create a list of at least fifty to one hundred tasks but the more the merrier here.

Keep in mind this is a one-and-done assignment. Once you have it, you simply update things here and there.

Be sure to list and not describe, which gives your 'secret sauce' away. For example, it is one thing to list: *Market on social media.* It's another to give your full strategy on Facebook because then they will not need you since you gave away all the details.

Put this in one column (but you will have a total of three for each letter of the acronym 'T.A.P.') and then total the number of tasks listed at the bottom.

The 'A' Stands For *Agenda*

Or, you can think of this second column as the time it would take for *someone else* to complete each of the tasks you just listed. This someone should not be a real estate professional like us, who has aids and resources to help. Instead, calculate the time it takes for 'Joe Blow' client, who does another profession for a living.

For instance, one task might be: 'Acquire the property legal description'.

For us as professionals, that may take all of five minutes to fire off an email to our preferred closing agent/attorney. Do not list that time.

However, 'Joe Blow' who again does not do this for a living may take several hours searching online for a suitable, affordable closing attorney/title agent and sending out feelers. List that in this column.

It may help to have a friend who is *not* a real estate professional try to do each of the tasks you already listed in column one to give you accurate estimates.

Total the number of hours for this column too.

Again, the total number of hours should be jaw-dropping. You are quantifying in writing that all of your efforts *do not* amount to just 22 minutes like on TV.

The 'P' Stands For *Price*

The client here gets to see the real cost of what you do if you do not (nor your company) have the vendor relationships and partnerships to default to using. Going back to our example with the task 'Acquire the property legal description', for you as a professional with a preferred list of closers, this is likely free.

Do not list that. Instead, list the cost that 'Joe Blow' would pay without a professional connection — likely the closing attorney's customary hourly rate, which could get into the hundreds, egad!

After you list the full prices for each task that non-professionals can expect and do pay, then total this column too. Many agents find that this equals more than their typical commission, which is when they are able to negotiate higher commission rates with the client in full agreement.

Now, take this finished document and give it some pizazz.

The top producers I work with have these three columns professional printed one time into a booklet. We *do not* give this book to clients to keep (remember, *do not* give away the secret sauce) but to solely review while in your presence. The details in the stylish printing make it less likely the client expects to keep it. If you have just a boring printout on regular white paper from your computer, prospects will probably accidentally stuff it in their purses because it just seems like an ordinary handout so jazz it up.

With the *T.A.P. into Your Value* principle, not only have I seen prospects understand an agent's value but more importantly, the agent, stands taller and prouder, having this visual document to solidify and memorialize all of her hard work. Newer agents gain confidence and veteran agents no longer feel intimidation from someone trying to strong arm them into not receiving what they are worth.

I challenge you to *T.A.P. into Your Value* this week (while this is still fresh and you have momentum).

Take the time to complete each column and watch not only your resiliency grow but your place in the real estate arena expand.

Here's to your success!

About Dr Lee Davenport

Armed with degrees in business and legal studies, Dr. Lee Davenport is an international real estate educator (as well as a former RE/MAX managing broker and agent). She has been recognized by Inman News and numerous real estate organizations as one of the top 25 US real estate coaches.

Additionally, Dr. Lee has article features in trade and consumer reads like REALTOR® Magazine. Remarkably, her doctoral research (studying the lead generation success strategies of top agents) is published in the peer-reviewed Journal of Real Estate Education and Practice -- in other words, she knows her stuff!

She is affectionately known for helping workshop audiences say, "Aha!" through her fun games used to explain essential technology, everyday business tasks, and how our God-given personalities can directly influence our level of success.

Contacts And Links

http://www.LearnWithDrLee.com

https://instagram.com/learnwithdrlee/

https://www.facebook.com/LearnWithDrLee/

and *#LearnWithDrLee*

lee@LearnWithDrLee.com

Mindset Matters

Mary-Anne Gillespie

I'm going to start with who I was. I came from a middle class family, and my parents taught me that the best thing that you can do is get a job with a pension pay off your house before you retire on a pension. I was fired from every job that I've had, was a C and D student, and I used to be 130lbs heavier.

When I was in high school, I had a guidance counselor telling me that I should take this test, and this test would determine what I would do the rest of my life. And the test said that I would be best suited answering phones and in order to achieve financial success in life I would have to marry "rich".

So I was like… "Alright, okay, I'll marry rich, no problem." I guess that's the best advice I got.

And then one day, my world got rocked apart when my mom died.

I was having breakfast one morning with my mom. I was just a kid. And later on that day, I got an emergency call that she was in the hospital. That story didn't end very well. I lost my family.

Shortly after burying my mom, there was police officers at my house. I was told I had ten minutes to gather my things and evacuate the house as it was not mine. I didn't know what was going on, I was so young.

To this day, all I have from that part of my life is two photo albums of my past family, as I like to call it, and cosmetic jewelry that my mom had; so that was all I was left with.

By the time, I was 24 years old, I had been through more things than I would wish on anybody. I couldn't get an apartment because I had no credit rating yet, not even a credit card. And so, I was homeless, and I lived in cars and surfed couches.

I went through probably the worst darkest place that you could ever go in your life. And thank God for the amazing receptionist that worked at the gym, which was where I showered and took care of myself who became my first roommate. I crashed on her couch until I could get on my feet.

Sometimes one of the key messages I want to also leave you guys is that homelessness is not always what you think it is. There are many people out there who just really have bad circumstances that they didn't choose, and they ended up homeless.

So that's a little bit about who I *was*.

Now, who I am today?

Today, I am the CEO of Red Apple Coaching an AMAZING Boutique Real-estate Coaching Company where we work with the top one percent of teams.

My second company is Gamechanger and I am launching my new passion company, GirlBundance. We will create the most fantastic mentorship program for business women world wide.

My first million was earned by 26.

I've been nominated businesswoman of the year, published several times in Forbes magazine, Real Estate Magazine (REM), and Inman.

I've shared the stage with Grant Cardone, Arlene Dickinson, and Ryan Serhant.

We work with over 800 of the top CEOs and business owners across the world with profits annually of over $2 million. We have a 98% success rate and a 97% retention rate.

And I've ran about seven marathons, did my first Ironman 70.3, and I'm doing three full Ironmans this year!

Importantly, I am a successful investor myself. I'd like to think I know a thing or two about the mindset that achieves success.

I share this *past-versus-present* picture because, too often, when growing up, we're told we can't. We are exposed to scarcity thinking by scarcity thinkers. Those thinkers can easily shape and influence our programming. We don't have a compelling purpose, we have a confused identity, faulty beliefs and often poorly formed values. We don't focus on the right skills and capabilities or behaviours. And worse we can remain bound by our circumstances or enviroinemnt. And then next thing you know we can't figure out - as adults - what has held us back.

In coaching we really work on discovering *abundance thinking*.

I've personally fought my entire life against the *scarcity mindset* and instead, have pushed through to abundance, daily.

I believe - truly, truly believe - I can do anything I want. Do you?

That's taken a lot of work. It's one of the reasons I chose to be a coach and love being a coach. Seeing potential in others, that was always there, but never discovered.

The one question that I'm asked consistently is, "How come that person over there is way more successful than I am? What are they doing that I'm not?"

Everyone thinks it's a process or system to follow and they expect to find some amazing formula they aren't following and it's the key to success.

I personally see something in our most successful clients that we call "Success Patterns".

They all seem to program their brain effectively whether intentionally or not.

Is it all in your head? It seems the way you think controls your thoughts, and those thoughts form habits. And those habits become your belief system and those beliefs create values. And then the values are what you produce in your world and your business and lives.

So yes, it ALL starts with your thinking.

95% of your actions are actually determined by habitual thinking. Meaning, what you've done the most of your entire life will give you the habits that have created what you live with today.

But... it can all be changed with new habits and new thinking.

I'm going to share my favorite success patterns that I believe are great foundations to achieving success!

Don't just do them once and forget about them, really be purposeful with how you decide to implement them and be 100% committed. When you go ALL IN on what you want you would really be surprised with how easy it is to get exactly what you visioned! I've seen it with over 800 clients. We've built over 100 new millionaires a year.

Use Your Imagination

First, use your imagination. The subconscious mind loves that. And the conscious mind is addicted to visualization, so, visualize where you want to go, and really *see* it.

I love neuroscience. It suggests that the subconscious

mind can't distinguish between what the conscious mind imagines and what's real. If that is true, and it is, give it positive sh*t every day and create amazing pictures of what is possible so the brain sees it!

I literally want you to daydream... and be as detailed as possible.

See the pictures in glorious colour. Make them big and bright. Make them *success* movies.

Then *feel* what it would be like.

Spend *at least* 15 minutes a few times a week just letting your mind create the picture of what you want. Choose to not watch TV for 15 minutes. This is the most amazing thing to do!

I remember visualizing walking on stage and speaking with Gary Keller (owner of Keller Williams) for years and out of nowhere, one day, I got an email from his team saying he wanted me to speak in front of 17,000 people with HIM. It was the most amazing experience and it was WAY better than I could imagine, by the way!

Always Keep Thinking Bigger! Intentionally.

Your brain doesn't know the difference between what's real and what's not. It believes what you tell it to believe. Always consider your thinking as intentional.

Think freaking epic sh*t. Think big. Think as high as you possibly can and feed your brain with it.

It doesn't know the difference.

Don't feed it the crappy stuff. Ever.

I also suggest that if you are wondering if you are truly thinking big then share your vision with some people who know you. If they don't seem a little shocked at your thinking and how big it is... you are underperforming. You want to really see your friends' faces go, "That's big! Wow!"

Then you know you are on the right thinking path.

Give Yourself Permission To Be Successful

A lot of people don't do that. We see that in coaching quite often.

We have clients who "want" to be successful but they just hold back. They can't give themself permission.

What does that mean? They feel they don't deserve it. Or they believe they aren't as talented as others. Or they aren't as ambitious. Or as outgoing.

They literally feel they need some permission to just GO FOR IT. The words *can* and *can't* are permissive verbs. *I can't* almost always means *I can't give my self permission to ...*

Your dreams are YOURS for a reason.

You can't have a thought that doesn't exist in your capabilities. When your brain gives you a drive or desire to accomplish something, that is your brain telling you something. You've accumulated thoughts since you were a child. Everything in you to accomplish that goal is possible. You cannot think what is not possible.

Okay, so people often think I have a crazy thought in my head. No, no, it's not crazy. It exists because it's possible. Stop comparing yourself to anyone else and just listen to what your own mind is telling you. It just might be telling you to go for it.

Don't Allow Other People's Fears To Cast Shadows Of Doubt

If you only knew, the amount of people that have told me that I couldn't do something; the amount of people who have kicked me when I was at my peak and said, *I want to take you down.* If you only knew all those type of people who have done that.

It doesn't matter. Nothing matters.

I don't surround myself with small thining negative people anymore. I surround yourself with epic people. Pay very close attention to this.

Surround Yourself With Positive Reinforcement

You want positive reinforcement. I've got some of the best people in my life, not a ton, but the best! And if it wasn't for them, I would never be where I am today. I wouldn't be here if it wasn't for my coaching clients. I never would have been published in Forbes magazine, I believed in me as much as they believed in me. What sets them apart is they are generous with their positive reinforcement. Avoid stingy people who withhold support.

Create A Vision Space

The brain works in pictures. On my vision board, I have a picture of a house in Hawaii that is not for sale. I see that house every day. I'm going to buy that house, I swear I'm going to buy it. And I know it. There's just like *not* even a doubt in my mind. It's going to be mine.

There is nothing worse than putting all your time an energy into chasing money. Chase fun, chase experiences, chase anything just put lots of pictures up and start attracting it! My vision board is kick ass, I love it. Create your own vision space and look at it every day. Don't do it because I say so; do it for yourself.

Identify Your Resistance.

A lot of people don't know what their resistance is. Trust me. It could be your circle of friends. Maybe they are saying stuff that feeds your self doubt. Or anxiety. Sometimes it's hard to know what our resistance is so we ask everyone around us. They can't know what it is. It's different for everyone.

But that's external. On the outside.

Internally, listen to your thoughts. That's on the inside. It's that little voice that is in your head that speaks out only right before we are about to take that first step off the ledge of comfort.

All you need to do is listen to what it is saying and then decide to never believe those words again.

But listen.

There are two schools of thought on shutting down negative self-talk. One is to listen to the *content* of that negative self-talk; and then dispute it. Prove it wrong.

The other is to simply ignore the content and notice the *volume*. Imagine a radio or TV with the volume turned up too loud. You'd simply grab the remote and turn the volume down or hit mute, right? Imagine the movie *Jaws* without the scary soundtrack.

Most negative self-talk actually has a loud volume!

Either way, external or internal, it creates resistance. Ultimately, resistance is your brain protecting you against anything unknown. That's its job.

However it shows up, pay attention when your resistance kicks in. Take some time to notice what holds you back so you can recognize it in the future. The only way to get on the other side of that is to get uncomfortable.

Start A Gratitude Journal

Once a day write down something you're grateful for. THAT will change your world.

I didn't look at the fact that I lost my family when I was young or that I was homeless, as a negative. I looked and I said, *You know what? Some people don't have great parents. I was lucky. I didn't have them long enough, but man, I had great parents and I had a great upbringing and knew love. That was a core foundation and some people can't say that and they've had parents for years, so you know what, that's what I'm freaking grateful for.*

My favorite thing is to know that when I have a really challenging day I'm still going to find at least one thing that was pretty amazing that I am grateful for.

It turns the perspective totally around. Gratitude and fear can't occupy the same space.

Release Your Attachment To The *How*

Perfection impedes progress. Surely you've heard of "analysis paralysis". That's where someone spends so much time focusing on the *how,* that they end up getting really frustrated with their slow progress.

Stop worrying about *how.* Jump in and figure it out later. The more risk you take the more it becomes a habit, and well, risk is necessary when you think big!

Fill Your Dead Airtime With Affirmations And Motivation

If you want your business to grow YOU have to grow. I am obsessed with keeping my brain sharp and exposed to different thinking. I love hearing new things even if some of them have nothing to do with my own business or life. There's empty space when I wake up in the morning, why not use that time to feed my brain some great things!

I have podcasts running all through my house in my car everywhere. My thought process is very intentional. Take advantage of walking your dog and put on a podcast. Listen to a book on your stationary bike. Have *clubhouse* in the background.

So although all this really appears to be easy changes... it's about *consistent* changes...

Remember we are building new habits and that's going to give us a new way of seeing things and thinking. It's what gives us the ability to have any life we want and create any success we want to have happen.

I have always known that anything is possible. History has repeatedly shown us that point. We get very frustrated when we "expect" to be somewhere and we aren't.

I know I am completely imperfect, I'm going to have bad days, distracted weeks, feeling of doubt, and feeling like I'm not progressing exactly where I want to be. But I always accept my role in what is currently happening.

Expectations can stop us from progressing.

The Gap is a place we get stuck in when we want to be in place A, but our reality is place B. It hits us like a wall. Unmet expectation is very hard to work through if you ignore it. It can be so disappointing and get in our way. It can really divert us.

It's because we end up working on our expectation rather than the actual tasks to what will get us the results. When you focus on your expectation, rather than the tasks, you lose all power and momentum in your goals.

Realize most difficulties are based on the expectations we have. How many times you have said, *This isn't how it's supposed to be?*

That just tells you that your focus is on expectations.

I suggest you take a pen, write down how it "should" have gone in a very detailed way. Then, what it looks like *now*. Aagin, very detailed.

Create a task list to get you *there* and let go of the expectation of where you are *now*, currently, and just live in this moment and focus on the tasks.

When you expect nothing, you are okay with today and can change anything you want. You own it!

Shift your mind and accept it!

My greatest reason for coaching is to really see people live their fullest potential. To not regret holding themselves back because of a mindset, belief system, or habits that have stopped them from being great.

I'll leave you with a quote, by Hunter S. Thompson, that I have in my office.

> *"Life should <u>not</u> be a journey to the grave with the intention of arriving safely in a pretty and well preserved body, but rather to skid in broadside in a cloud of smoke, thoroughly used up, totally worn out, and loudly proclaiming "WOW! WHAT A RIDE!"*

Dream Big Everyone!!!!!

About Mary-Anne Gillespie

At 23 Mary-Anne was one of the youngest VPs of Business Development for a large firm and recognized by the Ottawa Citizen as a "young business woman to watch". She was selected as the first coach to represent Canada with the #1 International Coaching Organization where she ranked as the top Business Coach out of 200 coaches all four years of her being there.

Mary-Anne is known for her ability to bring a record breaking number of businesses to top one in their fields. Currently her company, Red Apple Coaching and Consulting, works with over 700 business owners experiencing average profits of $3 million and 50% annual growth rates. In her free time when she's not studying Neurosciences, she runs Marathons, surfs the world, spears fishes and rescues puppy mill dogs and will finish her first full Ironman in 2021!

Contacts And Links

ceo@redapplecoaching.ca

redapplecoaching.ca

Unlock Your Best Life: Turn A "No" Into A "Yes"

Kat Drerup

I honestly lost count of how many times I failed the real estate exam.

Now I'm blinking in the mirror wondering how I'm in the top 1% of agents in Charleston, South Carolina after five years—and just turned 30. In the midst of a global pandemic, I doubled my volume and units. I formed a team and now mentor agents. Through cultivating relationships, I have grown a 100% referral-based and social-media driven business.

My highlight reel on Instagram appears pretty and seamless. My career may even look like it was handed to me on a silver platter with Veuve Clicquot sparkling in hand, but behind the scenes, I failed. I failed many, many times before I reached this level. There is no secret sauce to being successful, whether it be real estate or another dream you might have. It is simply finding a way to make a "no" a "yes." Through my story, I hope you find more "yes's" in your life.

My motto in life is simple: "Everything is figure-out-able." As a resilient woman in real estate, I have learned to figure it out. I look at failure and fear straight in the eye and give her a wink.

Six years ago I failed the real estate exam multiple times; and got laid off from what I thought was my dream job. This year, I formed my first team, and six months later the team member quit. For a second, I was a "team," party of one, while also selling a personal home, buying another and taking on all the repairs single-handedly. More than once, I dropped everything to show buyers property in a market that is equivalent to finding toilet paper in a pandemic. All while trying to write this chapter!

Needless to say, life happens.

There will always be challenges to overcome. If you want it bad enough, it takes time, grit and a "yes" from yourself.

So, my question to you: why wait for anyone else? Why wait until you have more time? Why wait until you're older or when you are ready? Why wait until you have more experience? Why stop if you have failed once, twice or even three times?

I am here to share my story while debunking myths about yourself. I am here to be your "yes" woman!

Like most stories, there are some behind-the-scenes details that you should probably know. Grab your box of popcorn and buckle up, I have shared these juicy details with very few people and I hope that in being vulnerable and genuine with you, that you can find the "no's" and turn them into "yes's" in your own life. It starts with commitment to yourself.

My thirst for real estate started during my dad's tenure in the Navy. We relocated to several homes across the country during my childhood. I loved tagging along for showings. I would bounce around in pigtails making suggestions like, "extend the porch," so I could jump off the deck into an (imaginary) pool in the backyard. As I got into my teens, I followed along largely to make sure that my room had a suitable closet. I was quite the diva about it, even at 13, so I can relate to all my clients that go straight to the closet during a showing. No judgement here!

As much as I cherish those showing tours with my parents, it was hard to start over as an only child. I moved into nine different homes by the age of 13. I knew first-hand what it was like to start completely over, feng shui a new room and make friends at a new school. Not to mention finding a new hairdresser (because we all remember that cringe-worthy haircut that made you get right down to business with finding the right stylist).

As an only child, I knew that if I wanted to sit with anyone at lunch, I needed to be confident enough to tap the kid next to me in homeroom class, introduce myself, and ask if they wanted to sit together and, perhaps, even throw out the idea of being best friends. I was forced to get out of my comfort zone, quick! I felt the pains and perils of moving to my core on so many fronts.

These moving experiences equipped me with the skills necessary to be my own boss, years later, and I didn't even know it. Confidence is one of the characteristics that has proven to be most valuable to me as a realtor. I am not afraid to be in a room full of people and not know a single soul. In fact, now I thrive on these experiences. I have the ability to empathize with my clients that are moving across state lines – or even just across town. Changes and new beginnings are difficult, even for the most seasoned individual. At the time, I didn't see the seeds that were planted for me to grow into the woman I am today.

Now, I am forever grateful for these challenges.

In 2013, when I graduated from the University of Georgia with a public relations degree, I would have taken any job. I was bright-eyed and bushy-tailed, ready to change the world. When I was offered a job in communications, I jumped at the opportunity and moved to Charleston, South Carolina.

The world was truly my oyster!

My parents helped me buy a house in Charleston (let's be real, my parents bought a house and added my name to the deed). My realtor's name was Darlene, and she was just as darling as her name. She was your typical 50-something fairy godmother that holds your hand through the whole process and makes the magic happen in a multiple offer situation. You can't help but to love and trust her right off the bat. She was a top producer in the Diamond Circle Club and sold properties on the beach. How glamorous!

She encouraged me to get my real estate license and said I had the "drive, determination and personality for it."

I thought, what the heck, at 24-years-old, I could use a resume-builder for my 9-5 job and perhaps, I could do it part-time or "just for fun." Plus, it was always a back-up career that sounded trendy when adults asked me what I wanted to be when I grew up. Truthfully though, I wanted to pursue a career in public relations and open my own PR firm one day.

After work ended each day at 5 pm., I would hurry home, change out of business clothes, grab a bag of chips and take night classes to obtain my real estate license. Well, almost.

Fast forward to the real estate exam. I failed it, again and again. I never told a soul except my parents and my boss. My boss finally had to know because I was taking so much "vacation time" each week that she was becoming suspicious.

It would have been easy to see my test failures as a big fat stop sign, hitting me square in the face, and to ultimately give up.

Instead, I saw it as a 4-way intersection; a temporary pause with three other avenues. In actuality, the stop sign was the momentum I needed to accelerate. It pushed me forward because the fear of failure was my fuel. There were other roads to travel to get to the same destination. After all, I am a "yes" woman!

It took me almost a YEAR to pass the real estate exam.

Do you know the craziest part about all of this? I wasn't planning to pursue real estate full-time. I just wanted to prove to myself that I could do it. I had a fire burning so fierce that I couldn't extinguish, and I had no idea it was so that I could shine bright for my clients later. I was resilient, unstoppable. You too have a fire!*

After two years of working in the communications job, I was recruited for my dream public relations job at a small PR firm. The job had all the bells and whistles: event planning, building relationships with influencers while launching grand openings at the hottest hotels and restaurants around town. I even had account managers and interns working under me. This was it! I had MADE IT—or so I thought. My world came crumbling down shortly after taking the position.

I remember the day vividly.

The CEO pulled me into her office on a Friday afternoon, shut the door, and apologized… I was being laid off. Evidently, the firm didn't secure the clients they needed to maintain payroll, and I had negotiated a larger salary than they could swallow. They asked me to gather my things and turn in my key. My jaw hit the ground in bewilderment.

For someone that was so ready to take on the world and change it for the good, it was a hard hit.

---

*The same boss that saw me fail the real estate exam multiple times is listing her house with me as of this very week. She knew that I was resilient, and now she knows I am unstoppable. If that doesn't give you chills and motivate you to keep going when life gets tough, then your goals aren't big enough!

In my head, I felt like they had fired me and "laid-off" was a nicer way of saying it. I took it personally. I replayed every meeting, every conversation, every step I took during my short time there. I started to question my worthiness and was so embarrassed that I had failed myself, my boss... and my career aspirations. I know it seems silly and totally irrational looking back at it, but I was seriously at one of the lowest points of my life. I felt that I had no purpose in life if I wasn't changing other people's lives. This was everything that (I thought) I wanted. I felt like I didn't even have a chance to make a difference or find my voice in the world before the door was shut in my face.

Based on the circumstances, it was evident that I found my identity in my job. I truly felt like I had lost a limb. "Devastated" did not begin to cover it. I wasn't the trendy "boss babe" that I had proudly posted on Instagram. In reality, I was the girl in her jammies, unemployed and sobbing into Ben and Jerry's Double Fudge Brownie ice cream.

My whole identity had been stripped away.

That is when I decided that nobody—no corporation, no entity, no boss, no person—was going to dull my sparkle again. I vowed I would never allow anything but myself to dictate my future. It was completely up to me to get out of my own way, put my fear of failure aside and put it all on the line. I can't describe to you how bright the fire burned inside me to hit the pedal to the metal and pave my own way. It was time to thrive with my own brand identity. It was time to shine with Kat Drerup front and center and, by default, real estate was the name of the game. I had to prove to myself that I could do this. There was no choice but to succeed. In fact, I was going to prove that PR company wrong and make double what they were going to pay me there.

But first, I needed business cards!

Enter in, Kat Drerup, the Charleston, SC Realtor. The first thing I did when I got into real estate was work on my brand, which is pretty strange to put as a top priority if you are new in the real estate business, but it was what I excelled at from my public relations background. I knew that I had to start at the beginning. Nobody knew the difference between hiring me or Suzy Q who has been in the real estate business for two decades. I was also two decades younger than Suzy Q, so I really had to prove my worth as a millennial in this business.

This is when I took my identity into my own hands and transformed it into something bigger than I ever thought imaginable.

I knew from my background in public relations that a brand is not simply a logo and unique colors. A brand is a feeling; it is the cape that makes you superwoman, or even the invisible cloak that protects Harry Potter. It is the "yes" woman you want people talking about. My brand was more than a newly-printed silky business card, it was my new identity. It was my elevator pitch without even saying a word. I wanted people to associate my name with THE Charleston Realtor® you can count on to have your back, like she would a best friend that sits with you at lunch when you are the new gal!

When I made the announcement that I was in real estate, most of my 20-something friends had very little knowledge about what I actually did. They would ask me countless questions about how the process worked. "How do I buy a home?" "What kind of financing do I need?" "What do you think I can afford?" "Wait, so I don't need 20% down?" There was always the encouraging, "I will definitely use you in five years when I am ready to buy my first house!"

The questions kept coming, so I began to strategize a plan to be an expert in my industry and fake it until I was it—pronto. I knew that I was merely a hobbyist until I proved to my friends otherwise. I needed to gain credibility, so I developed a strategy for a free First Time Home Buyer Seminar that anyone could attend.

This seminar was the single most important implementation that I used to accelerate my career. It ultimately took me to the next level because I created a system for hosting them every other month for an entire year. Years later, all the people that were first time buyers became first time sellers—and then buyers again. That is three transactions from one seminar! These free seminars doubled my volume and created raving fans.

Simply put, when you find yourself stopped at a 4-way intersection, see it as an opportunity with three different paths. Remember you are only stopped for a short period of time before you keep moving.

Turn your "no" into a "yes." It will lead you to places you never dreamed.

A Few Tips

- **Build Relationships, not Leads:** People work with who they know, like and trust. Assess how you can add value to those around you and arrive with a helping heart. These relationships are like planting seeds; you may not reap what you harvest in the same season. Relationships take time and you want to be a dependable resource.

- **Never Stop Learning:** Just because you start gaining momentum in your business does not mean that you are the expert. I set aside time every month to hop on a webinar, eLearning course or listen to podcasts that I can then apply to my business. These opportunities sharpen your skills and accelerate your systems as well as keep you up to date with industry trends.

- **Think in Abundance:** Lost in a multiple offer situation? Didn't get the listing appointment? It happens to the best of us. Every day is a new day—your highest high and your lowest low can happen on the same day in real estate. Try not to get down on yourself or question your worth. Keep moving forward.

- **Discover a Passion Outside of Work:** Select a passion that you can invest in outside of your career. My recent passion is dancing. It fuels my soul and gives me more energy to keep going. Discover what makes your heart sing. Mine is specifically, the tango.

- **Show Up on Social:** You don't have to use every social media platform known to man. Just pick one that you like that works for you. Stay consistent and maintain your own authentic voice that makes you relatable to your audience.

- **Favorite Book:** *Miracle Morning for Real Estate Agents* by Hal Elrod, Michael J Maher, Jay Kinder, Michael Reese, Honorée Corder

- **Favorite Podcast:** *The Goal Digger Podcast* with Jenna Kutcher - She gives tips and tricks for all industries and leaves you motivated to conquer.

I will leave you with my favorite quote that carried me through so many of my stop signs and speed bumps:

> *"Success is not final, failure is not fatal:*
> *it is the courage to continue that counts."*
>
> *- Winston S. Churchill.*

Everything is figure-out-able, my friend. There is no such thing as a "stop sign," it's a 4-way intersection. Go get 'em, sister! "I am woman, hear me roar!"

About Kat Drerup

Kat Drerup grew up in Athens, Georgia, but has been unlocking the dreams for homeowners in Charleston, South Carolina for five years. Kat has grown her real estate career from the ground up to become a top 1% REALTOR® in her market. Her signature First Time Home Buyer Seminars and captivating social media presence has grown her business into both real estate and coaching. Her degree in public relations and understanding of creative strategy has helped position herself as an industry leader and given her the ability to expand her booming brand into a team.

Kat is a Certified Residential Specialist, Realtor® of Distinction and member of the East Cooper Top Producers Club. She resides in Mount Pleasant with her dog, Sullivan, named after their favorite beach, Sullivan's Island.

Contacts And Links

Website

https://www.unlockchucktown.com

Facebook: Kat Drerup Carolina One Real Estate

https://www.facebook.com/UnlockCHS

Instagram: UnlockCHS

https://www.instagram.com/UnlockCHS

LinkedIn: Kat Drerup

https://www.linkedin.com/in/kjdrerup

Roadmap to Success

Kim Hayden

No journey worth taking is simple. It's bumpy and winding. However, with a roadmap you always arrive at the destination. A road map does not prevent life's inconveniences like storms and mechanical issues, but rather helps you arrive at your destination. You see, no matter how precise the path is, life happens. A map just ensures that when you are thrown off course you can correct and continue towards your goal, being resilient is the difference between reaching your true destination and settling close enough.

It took me a long time to find my road map.

I was born and raised in Wichita, Kansas, the oldest of four girls. My father was abusive (a story for another time), and we were always broke. Planning for the future was not a luxury we had. I learned very early on to react and deal with the most pressing issue of the moment.

By the time I was 20 years old, I had dropped out of high school, gotten married and subsequently divorced, and had a baby. I did manage to get my GED and my cosmetology license but I didn't really know what I wanted to do with my life. What I did know was that I was drowning in debt, medical bills were piling up, my electricity had been turned off and that I desperately wanted something more for my son.

But I didn't know where to begin.

Much like many other nights, I stretched out on the comfy devan mindlessly watching whatever was on TV with my grandparents, waiting until Johnny Carson started. This night featured a news segment on the economic boom in Las Vegas. It was the early 90s and Vegas was experiencing a period of unprecedented growth and people were heading there not just to gamble at the casinos, but to try and get a union job. You see, even waitressing jobs were unionized. They had guaranteed minimum wages, stricter work conditions and medical benefits. The thought that someone with my limited experience and education could ever have medical coverage, felt like winning the jackpot.

It didn't take much for me to decide that I needed to get to Las Vegas fast. Anything was better than where I was. I packed up the few belongings I had, jumped into my car and made the long journey from Wichita to Vegas. I only stopped for bathroom breaks, food and quick snoozes along the highway.

I didn't have a plan.

I managed to secure a waitressing job at Caribe Cafe at the Mirage working the graveyard shift, despite my lack of waitressing skills. My talent was talking. I loved to talk and listen to people's stories. Not necessarily a great quality for a waitress in the long run.

Cue the romantic music and enter my future husband - an unassuming, sweet Canadian in Vegas for work. He and two of his buddies had sauntered into the Cafe after a night out. He was smitten from the get go. I was more restrained.

Nearly a week before that fateful night, a fire broke out in my apartment, leaving me and my young son homeless. With nowhere else to go, we took up residence in my car. I had never felt so untethered and hopeless in my life as when that roof over my head was burned away.

But, meeting my soon-to-be husband opened my eyes and my heart to new feelings - not only love, but also security, safety and shelter. It was the first time I had really thought of what my future might look like.

So many possibilities opened up.

We were married within nine months in a small ceremony at the MGM in Las Vegas, to the tune of Somewhere Over the Rainbow, which was fitting given the ruby red slippers I wore.

We spent our honeymoon aimlessly driving up the California coast, taking in the sights and stopping when something caught our eye. It was such a fun and completely spontaneous trip, unlike any I had ever had.

We decided to settle in Toronto, as that was where my husband had been working for the past five years. The world seemed to open up before me. So many possibilities and options were available - maybe too many. I had lived for so long in a reactionary, survival mode that I floundered.

My husband encouraged me to apply for a job at an auto dealership, given my penchant for talking.

Within the first few months on the job, I was a top monthly salesperson, however it just didn't feel right for me. I wasn't really interested in cars. They were not my passion.

I left that job before Christmas and started my first entrepreneurial endeavor. I set up a kiosk at Queens Quay, a trendy harbour front area of Toronto, where I created custom holiday gift baskets. Sales took off, but was short lived, as it was a holiday-based business.

Yet again, I found myself at loose ends. I scanned the newspaper looking for jobs and came across a call for program directors at Jenny Craig. Within three months, I was moved into management.

This was where I really started to explore my collaborative mindset.

It was also the time that my family began to grow. We decided that maybe it was time to head to my husband's home city of Calgary.

Like so many times before, I packed up everything and made the cross-country move. Calgary was so vastly different than Las Vegas and Toronto. With its slower pace and quiet evenings, I had lots of time to think. I tried to throw myself into being a full-time mother, the hardest job I have ever had. I quickly realized that I missed people. We had moved into a newly developed community where I didn't know anyone.

Discontent to stay still, I put my people skills to work. I started a moms and tots program at the community centre to connect with other young mothers. When I wasn't tending to my two boys, I filled my time developing and growing that program. It quickly expanded and was eventually amalgamated into the homeowners' association programming.

After six months of being a stay-at-home mom, I realized I needed something more. While I loved caring for my children, I wasn't cut out for the job. My lack of a personal source of income left me feeling anxious. Having grown up watching my mother work three jobs while raising the four of us, I was compelled to seek something for myself.

In the summer of 1999, my husband said the infamous words, "Why don't you try real estate? It looks easy."

I thought why not. How hard can it be?

I spent the next four months studying for the real estate license exam, which I passed on my first try.

So far so good.

I joined Royal Lepage Foothills, the fastest growing brokerage in Calgary at the time. They offered an excellent training program plus, the woman that helped us purchase our home in Calgary, was an agent there and she spoke highly of them.

Along comes my first clients, a young couple looking to sell their small home so they could accommodate their expanding family. To have this family place their whole trust in me was such a surreal feeling - one that I had rarely experienced before. I was helping these two strangers make one of the largest financial decisions of their lives. I pushed my fear aside and delved in. The house sold in less than two months and the clients were happy. I was ecstatic. I was on my way!

As Kim Hayden signs went up in the neighbourhood and my business grew beyond a handful of clients, my fatal flaw became apparent.

I had no plan - no roadmap.

I had not put any systems or client tracking in place. I was inconsistent with followup. I operated from a sales person mindset, rather than a business owner one.

My 'system' consisted of file folders stuffed with papers and notes that soon became lost in a pile or at the back of the filing cabinet.

Something had to change.

Feelings of anxiety and guilt mounted as I worried that I had failed my clients. I continually had to seek out new clients rather than cultivating relationships with already established ones. It was exhausting and became a point of contention with my husband, and now business partner.

Doubt and insecurity crept in. I began to think that maybe I wasn't cut out for this work either - that maybe I would never truly succeed at anything. I had worked at so many different jobs - hair stylist, waitress, car salesperson, basket designer, ice-cream scooper, babysitter, manager, sales person. They all seemed so disconnected. Much like our honeymoon, I was aimlessly driving my way through life.

But that's when I had a realization. I had been building my map all along...

... I just didn't know my destination.

Each stop along the way, from Kansas to Calgary, sign posts and landmarks went up - things that I learned, skills I had built. But the map was incomplete. It showed where I had been, but not where I was going. I needed only to complete the map, and the first step to that was setting goals.

Over the next few years we continued to grow our real estate business. We hit every award level Royal LePage had to offer, up to the highest level, the Chairman's Club. When the Calgary Real Estate Board had the Million Dollar Award for Top Producers, we achieved this multiple times.

We became the first ICON team in Canada with EXP Realty in 2015, also receiving ICON two more times. In addition, we received the Alberta Centennial Award in 2005 for our community work and in 2012 again received civic recognition with the Queen's Diamond Jubilee Award. Through our community efforts as real estate agents we helped raised tens of thousands of pounds of food for the food bank, and became the #1 contributor to the Shelter Foundation, a foundation that helps women and children flee abuse.

After 22 years in real estate, I can look back with a sort of nostalgia at my naivete.

If I had only known then what I know now, as the saying goes. There are so many things I would do differently, the first being to find a business coach, mentor or accountability partner. I could have saved myself so much time, energy and tears had I been connected to someone that I could learn from, ask questions, hold me accountable, and guide me in creating a plan.

But the most important thing I have learned is about the need to be resilient.

When I look back, I never would have thought I would be where I am today. I could have ended up like so many other women that started where I did - broke in a trailer park in Kansas. I often say broken and broker are differentiated by one little letter, yet they are worlds apart. You may be broke today, but you're not broken. You are the broker of your own life and the creator of your own roadmap to success.

You can do it! I believe in you. *#realtorlife*

About Kim Hayden

From Kansas to Canada, Kim has always worked to be a good neighbor and leader. In every endeavor through Servant Leadership. Kim has repeatedly excelled in several industries. A 21-year award winning Real Estate veteran to over 1,500 minutes of TV Production.

Now bringing a lifetime of experiences and work together in the form of Real Resilient Tour, Kim is on a quest to bring the message of Resiliency and Leadership in unprecedented times. Self proclaimed Collaboration Queen, Kim admits to being an avid watcher, along side her grandparents, of Johnny Carson and aspires to be the host of incredible talent.

Contacts And Links

hello@resilientseries.com

www.realresilienttour.com

Instagram @resilientrewomen

Facebook KimHayden

Invest In Yourself

Resilient: the ability to have a past, without it dictating your future.

- Kim Hayden

Now that you are here, I hope you have found the kindred spirits and inspiration for you to get out of your way and step onto your path of greatness.

When you feel pushed and it would be easier to go with the good, keep in mind, good can block your great!

The rule of thumb is you are the sum of the five people you surround yourself with. Invest in yourself and others will naturally follow.

It is human to focus on our failures and forget to celebrate our successes, this is why the careful cultivation of your sphere is critical. Those around us will mirror back what we need to see when we need the encouragement to push forward.

We all question our skills and value from time to time, and wonder "Why me?"

I will ask, *"Why not you?"*

The world needs you!

Why not now?

Take time and invest in yourself, find the coach and mentor you align with. Expand to the next level, be it six figures, seven figures, building a team or moving into the coaching space.

> *Extraordinary people are ordinary people making extraordinary decisions.*
>
> *- Sharon Pearson, author of Disruptive Leadership.*

I would love to celebrate your successes along with you. Be sure to reach out IG resilientrewomen and our private FB group ResilientREWomen. Lets band together and support each other to go the next level.

> *"If you want to go fast, go alone.
> If you want to go far, go together."*
>
> *- African Proverb*

Resiliently Yours,

Kim Hayden

About Real Resilient Tour

Real Resilient Tour is a hosted platform that provides collaboration for industry and interest leaders. Our goal is to broadcast a positive message and actionable steps and to shine a spotlight on those who inspire and guide … to those seeking inspiration and guidance.

> *"If you want to go Fast, go alone.*
> *If you want to go Far, go together."*
>
> *African proverb*

The goal of Real Resilient Tour (RRT) is to GO FAR! WE invite you to spread the word of Resilience no matter who you are or what you do.

At Real Resilient Tour we appreciate the efforts it takes to put a cohesive and inspiring story together so our aims are to:

- Bring authors together to focus on their story in a highly curated platform
- Create relevant content that fits into today's busy lives
- Bridge the East coast to the West

- Unite global like-mindedness to counter the influx of negative messaging
- Inspire our audience to live their best life

If you'd like to connect visit *RealResilientTour.com* or email Kim Hayden at *hello@resilientseries.com*

Would You Like To Contribute To Future Editions Of Resilient Women?

I would like to take this opportunity to thank each and every contributor to this first edition of Resilient Women. It has been a fun, emotional and amazing process.

If you would like to know more about the Resilient Women and and get involved in the next release of our next Resilient Women publication then please connect.

We look forward to welcoming you into our amazing community.

To register your interest email Kim Hayden at

hello@resilientseries.com

Resilient Real Estate Women